LIFE
SAVINGS
CONVERSATIONS

Prepping You for the Ten Most Important
Money Discussions You'll Have in Life

AMY JAMROG

Published by Author Academy Elite
PO Box 43, Powell, OH 43065
www.AuthorAcademyElite.com

LCCN: 2020910686
ISBN: 978-1-64746-324-3 (paperback)
ISBN: 978-1-64746-325-0 (hardback)
ISBN: 978-1-64746-326-7 (eBook)

Amy Jamrog is a registered representative of and offers securities,
investment advisory and financial planning services through MML
Investors Services LLC, Member SIPC. Supervisory Office: 330
Whitney Ave., Suite 600; Holyoke, MA 01040. The Jamrog Group is
not a subsidiary or affiliate of MML Investors Services, LLC or its
affiliated companies.

DEDICATION

This book is dedicated to my Dad & Mom.

Dad, thank you for the
life savings conversations we shared as a family.
You were the person who taught me
the fundamentals of financial responsibility.
I have stewarded those lessons and passed them on
to countless people over the past twenty years.

Mom, thank you for showing our family
what it means to be generous.
You taught us to always share with others.
I carry your examples of kindness and love
into every life savings conversation I have.

Love,
AJ

CONTENTS

INTRODUCTION

It's rare to come across someone who inherently enjoys talking about money. For most people, the subject is loaded with emotion: worry, guilt, stress, shame, conflict, tension, and powerlessness—to name a few. And most of the feelings associated with money are negative.

But they don't need to be.

I have been a financial professional for more than twenty years. During that time, I've had the privilege of moderating thousands of conversations related to money. Many of them have been with married couples. Others were with an elderly parent and an adult child. Some have even included Mom, Dad, and all the kids in a family meeting. I've experienced the discomfort at the beginning of the conversations and the relief that comes at the conclusion.

The hypothetical stories shared throughout the book are meant to give you a glimpse into what individuals, couples, and families deal with at all different stages in life. These begin as conversations centered on your life savings: paying for college, how to handle money in your marriage, or what legacy you ultimately want to leave behind before you die. When handled with respect, transparency, and compassion, these conversations become life-saving:

- *That conversation wasn't nearly as bad as I thought it would be! I feel like my wife and I have such a better understanding of our priorities. It's a relief to know we're on the same page, and that we also share so many goals for the future. Even though we grew up differently around money, we are now able to create alignment and build our financial plan.*

- *I had no idea my parents would be so willing to talk about their plan with us. For decades, I've avoided approaching them about their money because I didn't want to offend them. Now we all have clarity about what they have and what their intentions are. I feel like a burden has been lifted off all of us. My siblings feel the same way.*

- *I'm so glad we have a plan for paying for college, and more importantly, that our son has a realistic expectation of what we can afford. Now he can be smart about where to apply, what's reasonable, and how we can approach the process together more practically.*

Throughout your lifetime, you'll be challenged by conversations related to money. Whether you're speaking with your young children about an allowance or your elderly parents about their end-of-life intentions, these conversations pertaining to some aspect of your life savings can create worry, awkwardness, and anxiety.

That's why I created this guidebook.

Too often, people jump into life savings conversations without properly preparing. I'll bet you've been guilty of this in the past. You've likely launched into a heated subject without warning, caught the other person off-guard, and left them ill-equipped to respond to your questions or ideas.

Maybe you've been on the receiving end of these unexpected questions and know how it feels to be taken off-guard. These spontaneous discussions spark defensiveness, insecurity, and typically reach no resolution. My intention is to provide guidance for you and your family so you can prevent this from happening anymore.

In this book, each chapter teaches simple ways to prepare for a specific "life savings" conversation. My goal is to share creative ideas and techniques, and then demonstrate how you can build skills to create your own clear, articulate talking points.

Being prepared to have a life savings conversation means taking the time to think about your intentions before you start talking. This book was written to help you approach your own life savings conversations with clarity and confidence. It will help you

> **THIS BOOK WAS WRITTEN TO HELP YOU APPROACH YOUR OWN LIFE SAVINGS CONVERSATIONS WITH CLARITY AND CONFIDENCE.**

create a plan to have more *discussion* and *resolution* with way less *argument.* You'll learn how to approach a conversation already having thought through potential feedback or pushback. You'll come across as more logical, more grounded, and less emotional.

But does it really matter?

Well, not if you and your fiancée are having a conversation about what to make for dinner. On the other hand, if you're about to discuss how much money to spend on your wedding versus eloping so you can save your money for a house down-payment, then yes, it definitely matters.

Do you need to be prepared and feel confident for a conversation with your spouse about planning for a summer vacation? Maybe not. But what about a conversation with your spouse about how much money to leave the kids in your estate plan? Not only do you need to be prepared, but you also might want some professional help in thinking through all the possibilities and pitfalls of this important discussion. That's what this book will help you do.

Life Savings Conversations is intended to help you think in advance about important financial

XII   LIFE SAVINGS CONVERSATIONS

conversations you're likely to have throughout your lifetime, to pose questions for you to consider, to get you more prepared, and ultimately to point you in the direction of a professional advisor if you need it.

Not Necessary but Helpful

Is it necessary to have a conversation with your daughter about money before she gets married? Maybe not. But could it be helpful? You bet.

Could some of these chapters help you avoid arguments and decrease resentment within your most important relationships? Even if the answer is *maybe*, wouldn't it be worth reading to find out?

Having money conversations throughout your lifetime is important and inevitable. Being more prepared and more confident increases your chances of having better outcomes.

I once met with a couple who had been married for twenty years. He had three children from his first marriage, and she had one. All four of the kids were grown. I asked them two beneficiary questions: How will your money get divided if one of you predeceases the other? And if both of you passed away, how do you see the division of the money among your children?

You might be surprised to hear that they *never once had a conversation* about who their beneficiaries would be if either of them passed away. I asked more specific questions: What if you both passed away? Would you divide all the inheritance evenly so that each of the four children received 25%? Or would his three kids share 50%, and her one daughter get the other 50%?

They *never once* had talked about this.

Needless to say it was an important conversation for us to have together, and it brought up all kinds of issues regarding family dynamics, which of the kids were more responsible, which kids were more in need, and how to treat future grandchildren in their planning. Imagine that for twenty years of marriage, they had not once had a fruitful, effective conversation about it. They didn't even know who the other had already named as beneficiaries in their retirement plans. And imagine the husband's surprise when he took a closer look and discovered that his ex-wife was still the beneficiary of his 401k plan because he had never updated the form at work after their divorce!

I'm not saying these conversations are easy. For most people, they aren't. What I'm saying is that it's much better to have tough conversations than to avoid them. My friend Paul said it best: "Conflict avoidance leads to damage control." *Does it ever.*

When you avoid difficult conversations, you eventually end up dealing with them later and often at a most inopportune time. For example, your mom is in the hospital, and you and your siblings are fighting about what you think Mom's wishes are for her end-of-life care. Unfortunately, Mom never put a plan together. Perhaps even worse, none of you had felt comfortable asking her about this when she was healthy.

This book is meant to create an awareness of the life savings conversations you will likely face at some point. It's also meant to help you think more proactively and confidently about these conversations before jumping in.

If you bought this book for yourself, then congratulations. Feel free to read it from beginning to end to bring awareness to many different subjects you'll eventually encounter. Or jump right to the chapter that applies to you now and start there.

Either way, give yourself credit for being willing to tackle these tough subjects.

If your financial professional, attorney, or accountant suggested this book for you, kudos to them for caring enough about you to help you prepare for your life savings conversations. You'll eventually thank them, or more likely, you'll be calling them to ask for their help in mediating some conversations for you and your family.

If your spouse, parent, child, or friend gave this book to you, thank them for caring enough to share this information.

My intention is that by reading this guidebook, you learn, become inspired, and, most importantly, take some action that ultimately changes your future. Let's get started ...

CHAPTER ONE

THE HEART-TO-HEART TO HAVE WITH YOURSELF ABOUT MONEY

You'll have plenty of opportunities throughout your lifetime to have money conversations with others. But what about the life savings conversation you need to have with yourself?

How much time have you honestly spent *with yourself* to think about and make decisions regarding your money?

Consider that you're already having some of these conversations, perhaps quite often in your head. In fact, you probably have chats with yourself about money every day.

Have any of the life savings conversations you've had *with yourself* sounded like this?

- If only I had a job that paid me more money, then I could ...
- I don't see how I'll ever get this (student loan, credit card, medical) debt paid off.
- Why didn't I start saving for retirement sooner?
- Why didn't I start saving for college for the kids sooner?
- I wish my parents taught me about money, then I might not be in this position.
- I wish I could go back to a time when my life was so much simpler and easier.
- I wish I knew more about money before getting married.
- I wish I knew more about money before getting divorced.
- Why didn't my parents plan better for their future?
- I should have kept my account separate from his. I have no privacy when it comes to my spending.

- Why didn't I make better spending decisions? I'd have more saved.

Notice a theme to these conversations? They're about wishful thinking, and they look backward. They're also negative. Not to mention that none of them are inspiring. In fact, these are all totally unproductive, often repetitive conversations. And we get stuck in these conversations even though we both know there's absolutely nothing we can do to change the past.

The Past

Review the list of unproductive money conversations from above. See how each topic looks backward? Each sentence references things you haven't done, wish you'd done, or wish had never happened at all.

Simply put, what happened, happened. And being aware of this concept can start to change your thinking when it comes to your money.

The next time you start to have a woe-is-me conversation with yourself, you're now going to hear a little voice remind you: *This is a conversation from the past, about the past, looking backward on something that already happened. Stop it. What happened, happened. There's nothing you can do about it. It's time to move on.*

Pay attention and notice what happens as you move forward. You'll start to become annoyed by those old conversations rather than get sucked in. You'll realize

> YOU'VE GOT TO START THINKING: *ENOUGH ABOUT THE PAST.*

they don't help you and don't propel your life forward at all.

You've got to start thinking: *Enough about the past.*

The Present

What's far more powerful is focusing on your present situation. The life savings conversation you want to have with yourself begins where you are right now.

When you think about the timeline of your life, consider for a moment that it begins today. And frankly speaking, it ends when you're dead. Let's assume you have a lot you want to accomplish between today and the end. You'll have plenty of time to fulfill your dreams, complete bucket list items, make a difference for yourself and others, and create a legacy you'll remember when your life is ultimately over.

To accomplish these things, you may want to create a more mature relationship with money. How do you do this? Start by recognizing the difference between facts and feelings.

When it comes to money, you need to acknowledge the powerful role your feelings continue to play. For example, you may find yourself getting bummed out about the negative, stressful, anxiety-provoking feelings you have about money. This is common.

It's also totally unproductive.

When this happens, it's difficult to look at the *facts* of your situation and figure out what to do next. When feelings are running the show—especially the negative ones—it's hard to come up with a productive game plan to get you unstuck.

Try this out. Think about a money situation you have negative feelings about. For the next minute, close your eyes and step back so you can look at your situation as if you were an observer of your life. Ask yourself, *What is this emotion I'm feeling right now?*

Take Michelle as an example. She was complaining to me one day about her credit card debt:

> *It's just so frustrating that I have credit card debt I can't seem to get rid of. I feel like no matter how hard I try the $10,000 balance never goes down. I'm annoyed that it negatively affects my credit score. I wish I didn't have this ridiculous payment every month. I could be doing so many other things with my money. And it's not even like I have something good to show for the bills. It's just a ton of little purchases I probably shouldn't have made from a long time ago. And I'm still paying the price every month, plus interest. I'm so tired of it. And I can't seem to get rid of it.*

Michelle's money conversation is negative and backward-looking. In this circular conversation, she keeps faulting herself for things she purchased in the past. Her feelings are very strong. And no matter how many times she rehashes the past, it's not helping move her forward in any positive way.

Instead of giving her feelings so much credit, she could begin focusing on the facts. By reframing the conversation, she might be able to notice how her narrative about her *annoying, frustrating, resentful credit card debt* is set in the past, and this time decide to do something about it.

Like Michelle, when you reach the pivotal point where you get tired of listening to yourself talking about the past and getting into action to change your situation, you realize your feelings are basically irrelevant.

All of Michelle's feelings, strong as they might be, did not prompt her to do anything different to change her situation. She needed a game plan. She turned to her financially savvy friend, Brett, for help. Brett helped her with her budget, discovered places she could save money each month, encouraged her to cancel useless subscriptions, and identified expenses she could cut back temporarily. When each of these facts became clearer, Michelle took that extra *found* money and beefed up her monthly credit card payments to erase her debt much sooner.

When you realize your feelings are not relevant, you start to see how focusing instead on the facts can be so much more productive. This is when you begin to have a more mature relationship with money.

Like Michelle, Bradley was also stuck. His life savings conversation with himself was similar, weighed down with emotions and feelings:

> *I can't believe Sherry spent so much money on Christmas again. Every year, no matter how many times we talk about it, she just keeps getting caught up in the "magic" of the holiday season. The sheer volume of presents sitting under our tree on Christmas morning for the kids is embarrassing. They don't need that much stuff. No kid needs that much stuff. They certainly don't appreciate it. And what's even worse is I start to resent the entire holiday season in January once the bills come in because I'm the one who has to pay for it all.*

Bradley was annoyed, mad, embarrassed, and resentful during what's supposed to be the most wonderful time of the year. Sadly, this was not a new holiday experience for him. He and Sherry went through this every year.

Bradley needed to practice putting his feelings aside and stop focusing on what hasn't worked in the past. He needed to focus on the facts. He decided he would get into action proactively now for *next* Christmas and sent Sherry an email to suggest they set up a Christmas savings account far in advance of December. Sherry, not caught up in the holiday spirit since it was only spring, agreed with his idea. They decided to make a plan. They worked out their budget and determined an amount of money to deposit into the new account systematically on the 15th of each month starting in May. They agree that whatever was in that account by December was what they would spend on Christmas shopping. Period.

This proactive choice provided clarity on the budget. Sherry became more thoughtful and deliberate about the gifts she bought the family. With fewer presents to distract them, the kids were more appreciative of what they received for Christmas. Bradley enjoyed the holiday season knowing that Christmas has been pre-funded, which meant no post-holiday resentment because he no longer had January Christmas bills to pay.

You might be thinking that this solution is *so obvious,* and they should have resolved this much sooner. That is easy to say as the outsider looking in. Sometimes it's too hard to separate feelings from facts when it comes to your money. Couples get stuck trying to change spending habits, address old patterns of behavior, and deal with their feelings. Sometimes it seems impossible to come up with solutions that were hidden from your view due to all the emotions cluttering your path.

Moving on

At this stage, you might be thinking about some old money conversations you've been having with yourself that are focused on the past. Hopefully, you'll look for reminders to stop yourself when you start to get sucked in and instead focus on the present. You'll begin to recognize how strong your feelings are and start focusing instead on putting irrelevant feelings aside when they don't propel you forward. These are all things to practice. The good news is that you have opportunities every single day to try out this new approach.

And now, you're ready for a more evolved life savings conversation with yourself about your incredible future.

The Future

Have you ever sat down quietly on the couch, gone out for a run, or meditated silently and asked yourself any of the following questions?

- What role does money play in my life now?
- Is this the role I want money to play in the future?
- What old money conversations have I inherited from my family that I'd like to eliminate from my thinking moving forward?
- What kind of life would I like to have, starting today?
- Based on the life I want to have, what must change?
- What do I need more of in the future?
- What do I need less of in the future?
- What kind of retirement lifestyle do I dream of?
- What is on my bucket list?

- Do I even have a bucket list? Is it written down? What do I want to check off next?
- Where are all the places in the world that I'd like to travel to in my lifetime?
- What bands do I want to see in concert?
- Which sporting events do I want to go to?
- Which Broadway shows do I want to experience?
- What kind of life do I want to provide my child(ren)?
- What kind of support would I like to provide my _____ (parent, sister, cousin, friend)?
- What charitable organizations am I passionate about?
- What issues exist in the world that I'd really like to fix, improve, or eradicate?
- When it comes to money, what would _enough_ look like?
- When it comes to money, what does _generous_ look like?
- When it comes to money, what does _abundance_ look like?
- What does _being wealthy_ look like for me?
- Am I in a job that pays me what I am worth?

- Am I doing work that I love?
- What am I doing that makes a difference for me?
- What am I doing that makes a difference for others?
- Could I give away 5% of my income to someone or someplace?
- Could I save 5% more of my income for the future to make it better and feel more secure?
- If I died yesterday, would there be clear instructions for my loved ones today regarding my final wishes?
- Do the beneficiaries of my accounts, investments, and life insurance reflect my current wishes?
- What *are* my current wishes?
- If I die young, what do I want to make sure I accomplish/do/see before my life is over?
- If I live a long and fulfilling life, what else do I want to make sure I do/see/accomplish before my life is over?
- What has to change on my calendar *this year* to get into action?

- What has to change on my calendar *this month* to get into action?
- Who can I ask to help me with this?

Start at the top and work your way down this list of questions. Have a life-savings conversation over a quiet cup of coffee, while out walking your dog, or on your drive home from work. Keep your focus on the future you want to have. Brainstorm. Dream.

KEEP YOUR FOCUS ON THE FUTURE YOU WANT TO HAVE.

Write. It. All. Down.

Once you get comfortable having life-savings conversations with yourself, you'll be able to expand them to include others. Give yourself the freedom and space to create a new future for yourself. Then, start to share your ideas. Tell your spouse, your parents, your colleagues, and your kids about the amazing things you've planned for yourself and them. Create your bucket list and tape it to the refrigerator to remind you of it every day. Then, ask a friend, a spouse, or even a financial professional for some accountability to turn these wonderful ideas into your reality.

CHAPTER TWO

TALKING WITH YOUR CHILDREN ABOUT EARNING, SAVING & SPENDING MONEY

Before you can talk with your kids about money, you and your spouse will want to have a conversation with each other.

Keep in mind that each family has different personalities and dynamics to contend with, such as divorce. And every child is unique. That's why it's so important for parents (and ex-spouses, when possible) to get on the same page and decide how it's going to go.

Ask yourselves the following questions:

- What did your parents teach you about money when you were growing up? Is that what you want to teach *your* kids?
- How was money valued in your house growing up? Was money abundant or scarce?
- Were you expected to do chores? Did you get paid to do them, or were you expected to pitch in as part of the family's household responsibilities?
- Did you get paid an allowance as a kid? If yes, what did it teach you? If not, what did that teach you?
- How is money handled in your household now?
- Would you say you are doing a good job managing income versus expenses and making smart choices for your family? If not, what needs to improve?
- If you could fast-forward thirty-plus years, what would you want your kids to say that they learned from their parents (you) about money when they were younger?

These Can Be Tough Questions

Parents also wonder, *Are we supposed to be paying our kids an allowance? How much is the right amount to give them? When should this start?* Paying allowance to children is an opportunity for parents to teach the value of money, what it means to work hard and to be rewarded financially, and what it means to save for something you want.

But the subject of paying allowance is not clear-cut. In fact, you might not like the concept at all. Are you wondering: *Am I really supposed to pay my child to make his bed and set the table for dinner? Shouldn't he do that anyway, given he lives here for free?*

These are great questions. And they lead to a more philosophical conversation about what you want your kids to learn from you about money. Often this gets muddied by how your past experiences with money have shaped who you are today and how you still use that information to make financial decisions in the present. When children come into the picture, you start to see how growing up differently from your spouse can be challenging when you have to align on money decisions that will affect your future and your children's futures.

This challenge is very common between spouses: opposites attract, right? Coming from opposite backgrounds can also cause tension when it comes to money decisions and learned behaviors. This is where couples can continue to look for opportunities to create new patterns and traditions to benefit the family.

Where Do You Begin?

Know what you are dealing with and set expectations. Some children are good at saving, others are excellent at spending. Some parents are very responsible about money; others not so much. No matter how you've dealt with money in the past, and no matter how good or bad you are about managing your cash flow, you now have an opportunity to start fresh with your children. Kids can learn valuable, lifelong lessons from you about money.

To help you get started, here are a few ideas to ponder before you have a life savings conversation with your kids:

Consider Separating Chores from Allowance

John and Katie's kids were six and ten when they started giving them a weekly allowance. They took on the philosophy that as grown-ups have jobs for which they get paid, so do kids. For example, parents go to work, do the tasks they are responsible for, and then, at the end of the week, parents get paid for doing their jobs.

John and Katie explained to their children that it's their job as children to be good students and good citizens. If they worked hard in school, paid attention, did their best, and were kind to their friends, they were doing great at their job. And for that, they were going to receive a weekly allowance.

The kids were thrilled! It seemed to them that they just needed to keep being kids, *but now they'd get paid.*

The kids quickly learned that there was more to it. John and Katie explained that separate from doing their job of being good students and good citizens, the kids were also expected to do chores around the house but *not for money*. As John explained to the boys, "Separate from Mom and me going to work and earning money, we also cook dinners, provide a safe place for you to live, and make sure you both have clean clothes and fresh sheets on your beds every week. That is our responsibility. And we do these chores at home *even though we don't get paid*. As for you kids, doing your part means you're going to be responsible for setting and clearing the dishes every night, making your bed every morning, and putting away your clean laundry every week." And this became their new household standard.

Consider Paying Your Child an Allowance in an Amount That's the Same as Their Age

John and Katie's kids are six and ten. This would mean that they receive six and ten dollars, respectively each week. You might be thinking that's too much money for kids to be spending. Here's what's important to teach: The kids will not keep all of it. They'll first save some for college, then some for charitable donations, and then they'll be allowed to spend what's left.

John and Katie added their own *bonus* program: When each child had a birthday, they received a raise of one dollar more in their allowance. Again, John and Katie decided to link the kids' job of being a good student and citizen to earning a weekly allowance. And the older they got, the more they were paid.

Why the annual raise? The parents explained that continuing to be a good student and a good citizen can often get harder as you age. But if the kids managed to do that challenging work, it would be worth more money to them.

Continue to develop your family's version of this conversation. You might be amazed by what you all learn and the profound questions that your children might start to ask. Maybe you choose to pay an allowance every other week or match the kids' allowance with the same days that you get paid. What you choose is up to you. Just be *consistent*.

When Paying Allowance to Your Children, Consider Using Actual Dollars (Not Digital Payments)

If you want your kids to connect money they earn with how much things cost, it can sometimes be more effective to use real dollars when you pay their allowance, especially when they are first learning these concepts. You can make this a fun family project. You could even build this conversation into a family meeting.

Here's how John and Katie did it: To start, they gave each child three separate envelopes. They showed them how to label them for spending, donations, and college savings. The kids took time also to draw pictures and decorate them.

Then, their parents explained what each envelope was for and why. The kids learned that their allowance would get divided three ways. To keep it simple, John and Katie decided that the kids would keep 50%, give away 25%, and put 25% in their college envelope.

When the donation envelope started getting full, they asked questions to help the kids think about ways they could give those dollars away: *Do you care about the local animal shelter? Is there a family you'd like to help over the holidays? Would you like to donate books to your library?* Maybe in your family you give money to your church each week. This is where you and your children can start to define your values and match dollars to what you and the kids care about.

When the college envelope got full, John and Katie explained to the kids that this cash would be deposited into their college funds. This might also a great time to set up 529 College Funds for your kids if you haven't already. Check out the options for your state to choose the plan that makes the most sense.

As for the spending envelope, this is a great opportunity

CONSIDER THAT YOUR CHILD'S SPENDING CHOICES SHOULDN'T BE ATTACHED TO YOUR OPINION.

to let your child decide whatever it is he or she wants to buy. The challenge for parents is to not advise about what they consider is a good or a bad purchase. *Consider that your child's spending choices shouldn't be attached to your opinion.*

Allowance is about letting your son or daughter start to see the value of earning, saving, and making his or her own decisions about how to spend their money.

Let's say your son wants a Lego set and it costs $20.

What if he gets $2 per week for his spending envelope? If the Lego set costs $20, this is where you have the opportunity to teach him that he will need to wait *ten weeks* to save up enough money to buy it. Let him decide if a particular purchase is really worth it. It may or may not be—but try to keep your feelings to yourself as he figures this out.

For John and Katie, their six-year-old spends everything he earns every week. Two dollars does not go very far. Conversely, their ten-year-old has much more patience, sets goals, and can save for months. In fact, he saved for twenty-five weeks to buy himself a $75 scooter. He was so proud when he went to the store and paid for it with his savings.

The *spender* little brother witnessed this very exciting purchase and claimed it wasn't fair that his brother got something so awesome. This was an excellent lesson for both of the kids to learn.

Take the First Step and Plan a Weekly Family Meeting Time

Talking with your kids about money as a family and taking the time each week to divide the dollars into the envelopes then giving them raises each year can be incredible lifelong lessons for you to teach (even if you didn't learn them yourself growing up).

When you give your kids a weekly allowance and then offer them the freedom and flexibility to make good (or not-so-good) decisions with their money, you are setting them up for a very different future than they might have had.

What if your parents had done this for you? What kinds of decisions would you have made differently in your teens or twenties?

The earlier you start teaching your children these skills, the better. Imagine what they'll know by the time they start their first jobs as teens if they learn some money basics at six and ten years old.

Keep in mind that it's never too late to model these behaviors. Maybe your kids are teenagers, and you didn't do this when they were younger. Do they work and earn money? You can still teach them to spend some, save some, and donate some. While they live in your home, you still have an opportunity to teach your children values, habits, and skills. *It's never too late.*

Setting up savings accounts, establishing college funds, and even teaching your children about investing are great reasons to begin a life savings conversation.

Down the road, when your child successfully graduates from college and begins his or her first job, you can explain the basics of employee benefits, show them how to choose their 401k investments, as they take their first steps toward building their financial future.

CHAPTER THREE

TALKING WITH YOUR TEEN ABOUT COLLEGE

Before jumping into this chapter, keep in mind that not every child is interested in or planning to attend college.

But if your child intends to pursue education beyond high school and you intend to help pay for it, it's important to know that your family's strategy to pay for college is a *math* conversation.

This is not about your pride or your feelings.

This is also a conversation you should consider having before your child has even begun looking at colleges. Don't underestimate the impact of having it with your teen. Few parents are willing to have this conversation or don't know how to begin. After reading this chapter, you'll feel more prepared to have a proactive life savings conversation with your high schoolers about their college application process and ultimate choice of school.

And although this chapter refers to a traditional four-year college, you can easily substitute trade school, community college, or starting a business—these are all choices your child might be considering, and they'll all take some planning.

Many parents' goal is to pay for college for their children. Often their parents did that for them, so they'd like to provide their kids with the same benefit. Conversely, if they didn't have financial support from parents, and instead took out loans to pursue their education, they often conclude later that they don't want to put their kids in this position.

The student loan burden in our country is a gigantic problem. Throughout my career, I have worked with highly educated, responsible people who have great jobs, earn significant income, and really want to save for their future, but they've racked up tons of student loan debt. This creates tremendous stress and almost always creates resentment. In virtually every case, their stress can be summarized by one of these statements:

- *I wish someone would have told me how burdensome this would be. I would have made different choices. I never would have borrowed so much.*
- *I want to save for a house down payment, but these student loans are taking up all of my extra income. I wish someone would have told me about this when I was younger.*
- *I make good money, but with my student loan payment being so high, my credit score sucks. I wish I would have known the snowball effect that these loans would have on my life. I would have chosen a state school.*
- *I need to save for retirement as well as my kids' college education. But because of my student loans, there's only so much money to go around. I don't think it's possible to afford to do it all. I don't know how to get ahead.*
- *Help me figure out how to save money for my kids' education. I don't want to put them*

*in the same position I was in. It took me for-
ever to pay down my loans.*

Student loan debt is burdensome and stressful
and sets people back years (if not decades) from
achieving their goals.

With some basic understanding and a will-
ingness to have candid conversations with your
children *in advance*, you can potentially avoid
repeating this pattern.

Take the Smithfield Family. Randy and Rena had
their daughter, Piper, when they were in their late
20s. They proactively saved money for her education since the time she was born. By the time
Piper entered her junior year of high school, her
parents had accumulated $70,000 in a 529 College
Account. It seems like they did a great job, right?

Maybe ...

It's what happens next that matters and whether
the parents choose to be reactive (a common
reaction to planning for college) or proactive
(where the outcome could be so much better for
everyone).

The Reactive Scenario

When parents take a reactive approach to the college process, it can go something like this: Randy and Rena tell Piper to do some research and create a list of all the places she'd like to attend. Then, they take her on the campus tours based on places she picked. Based on her GPA and her desire to study veterinary medicine, Piper identifies six schools she's interested in. She applies and is accepted at four. All of them cost between $55-70K per year. And it's a five-year program, not four. She chooses a mid-level school for $60,000 per year. Her parents only have $70,000 in total saved for tuition and are unable to contribute more. What does this mean for Piper?

- POSSIBLE BAD OUTCOME #1: Piper graduates from the veterinary program in five years and ends up with $230,000 in student loans at age twenty-three (five years of tuition at $60,000 a year minus the $70,000 from her parents). Her monthly student loan payment will be almost $1,400. Her loans will be paid off at this rate in twenty years. And this is before Piper considers grad school.

- POSSIBLE BAD OUTCOME #2: Piper starts to realize in her sophomore year that choosing a $60,000/year school was a terrible financial decision. She hears about how burdensome student loans will be after she graduates. She doesn't want this for her future. She sadly and reluctantly drops out after her sophomore year. She has spent $120,000 in tuition minus the $70,000 from her parents. That leaves her with a student loan of $50,000. She transfers to a state school for $20,000 for the next three years to finish her program (another $60k student loan). Piper is left with $110,000 in student loans. She also is left with disappointment and regret that she couldn't have stayed at her first-choice school. But most disappointing is that her student loan payment at 4% interest is $665 a month for twenty years.

Are you starting to see a pattern here? Consider that it could be even worse:

- POSSIBLE BAD OUTCOME #3: Piper gets accepted to the $60,000/yr. school. Her parents feel terrible that they didn't save more for her. They don't want to burden her with huge student loans. Instead, they spontaneously decide to refinance their house and borrow $220k home equity to pay for tuition ($300,000 tuition, minus their savings of $70,000). In this scenario, Piper graduates with no student loans. What's the bad news? In their refinancing, Rena and Randy increased their mortgage payment by $1,400 for the next twenty years—a mortgage that was on track to be paid off by their age sixty-five. They educated Piper, but now they will not have the retirement they dreamed of.

None of these scenarios are ideal. That's because they were all reactive emotional approaches. What if instead, Randy and Rena—along with Piper—took a more proactive and less emotional approach to planning and paying for college?

A More Proactive Scenario

What if it went more like this?

Randy and Rena sit down with Piper after her sophomore year of high school. They explain to her that they've saved $70,000 for college. They discuss their commitment to her continuing education. They also recommend that she look at schools that fit into the $70,000 total budget. This is new information for Piper. *But since she hasn't even started the process yet, she isn't attached to any outcome. She hasn't toured any schools. She doesn't have her heart set on anything.*

Piper does some research. But in this more proactive scenario, Piper knows she needs to limit her search options by price. She finds several schools offering veterinary medicine as a major and all for in-state tuition. She gets excited about her choices. Many of the schools actually seem terrific to her.

She and her parents tour six of the state schools, and Piper is accepted to four.

- POSSIBLE AWESOME OUTCOME: Piper chooses her top choice. Tuition, room, and board are $20k a year. On a five-year program, the total cost of Piper's college will be $100k. She decides to work full-time in the summers and earns plenty of money to pay the difference. She graduates in five years with no student loans. Her parents don't need to remortgage their house, nor do they feel compelled to take out loans to support Piper's dream of going to college. They did exactly what they could afford. Piper ends up educated, happy, and debt-free.

See how a proactive approach can help get everyone involved and clear at the beginning of the process?

These can be challenging conversations to have. But if college is on the horizon for your child, the following three discussions should take place in this order:

#1: You and Your Spouse Talk with One Another First.

The two of you need to be on the same page before you involve your child in the conversation. Or, if you are divorced, you and your ex-spouse, if possible, should try to get aligned.

Ask yourself and one another:

- What's our college savings philosophy?
- Do we want to pay 100% for college? At what cost? Even if it means postponing our own retirement goals?
- Do we want our child to have some skin in the game and be responsible for a portion of the tuition?
- Do we believe that private school is important? Is a private school education going to put our child in better long-term shape in terms of his/her career?
- Do we feel like a state school can give our child a solid foundation for half the cost of private school?

#2: Consider Reaching Out to a Financial Professional if You Need Help.

An advisor can help you to determine:

- What you can afford to save for college.
- The best strategy for paying (home equity, 401k loans, 529 college accounts, federal vs. private loans, from cash flow, etc.)

- An understanding of what is realistic for you to pay and what you might be willing to change in your plan, if necessary, to make it work.
- What you are willing to sacrifice.
- Perhaps more important, whether your sacrifices will really make an impact on your child, their education, and your financial future. Together, you'll be able to determine: *is it worth it?*

#3: Lastly, Take the Time to Sit down and Talk Candidly with Your Teen.

There are no *right* answers. Your job is to balance your feelings and your philosophy with your resources. You may have grand plans to pay 100% for your daughter to go to your alma mater. But if you can't afford to save for your retirement, this pipedream is probably unattainable or downright silly to pursue.

I know. It's a hard conversation to have, but this is one that can save your family *a ton* of stress, worry, and

HOW YOU CHOOSE TO HANDLE THIS COLLEGE PROCESS COULD IMPACT—POSITIVELY OR NEGATIVELY—THE NEXT TWENTY YEARS.

wasted money on years of student loan interest payments. How you choose to handle this college process could impact—positively or negatively—the next twenty years.

Before you begin the college shopping process, and before you take the first tour or buy your child a sweatshirt at the college bookstore, have a candid conversation:

- Be clear about your resources. That includes what you can afford to pay and what is realistic in terms of institutions they're considering.
- Discuss the impact of student loans and what it means to both the student and the family if either of you borrow money for college.
- Explain your philosophy about paying for college. Can you pay for it all? Will they be responsible for some? If you are divorced, what have you and your ex decided?

This is where you may need to put pride aside to get real. If you have saved $70k for college, it would not be wise for your child to tour a $70,000 *a year* school, unless he or she is wildly talented, plays an unusual sport or instrument, or all of those things simultaneously, and is likely to be recruited or receive a full scholarship. And you cannot bank on this. Be proactive. Otherwise, you and your child are looking at the inevitable, significant student loan debt upon graduation for either or both of you.

It's not unusual to see parents take out loans for their children's education *while still paying for their own student loans.* As you can imagine, it makes it challenging for anyone to get ahead post-graduation. This is one of the biggest reasons why there are so many highly educated, smart twenty-somethings still living at home—their jobs don't pay them enough to be able to afford student loan payments plus rent and insurance and food and a car payment. The math doesn't add up.

And if you're the parents who dreamed of one day being empty nesters, this can be very stressful on your marriage. I know a couple who, at their most stressful point in marriage, had all three of their kids back home. Believe me, this was never anyone's goal, and neither was the $1,500 monthly grocery bill during this eighteen-month extended family reunion.

Begin by talking with each other. Then, sit down with your kids. Be real. Be patient. Be clear. Give your son or daughter the opportunity to see how much better off they could be by taking practical and proactive approach to their college search process.

CHAPTER FOUR

THE CONVERSATION TO HAVE BEFORE GETTING MARRIED

Let me preface this chapter by saying there are many romantic reasons to get married. I'm not arguing that. But there are also some very practical things you need to consider before tying the knot. Lovebirds—especially the younger they are—don't stop to account for what it means financially, legally, and tax-wise to get married.

Take Tom and Claire for example:

Tom and Claire had been dating for two years. They were twenty-five years old, both with college degrees and decent jobs. They lived together in a nice apartment but dreamed of one day buying a home. They sat down one night after dinner to figure out how much money they needed to save each month for a house down-payment. They wanted to know how long it would take to save realistically for a home and what they could afford for a mortgage. Sounds responsible, right?

While this was happening, Tom was struggling with something and didn't know how to tell Claire. Of course, he shared her same dream of owning a home, but he also knew he would soon need to buy a diamond engagement ring. He recalled Claire's big expectations for the ring (which she had mentioned on more than one occasion). In addition, Claire hoped for a fancy wedding and was planting the seed with her parents to try to get a sense of how much they were going to spend eventually. Tom and Claire had competing financial goals, and neither knew how to prioritize or sort them out together.

Having Financial Goals That Are in Competition with Each Other Is Common

Do you buy a house first, or do you buy an engagement ring? Should you splurge on an expensive wedding or earmark that money for the house down-payment? These were only a few of Tom and Claire's financial questions. There were plenty of others:

- Although they'd been together for two years and jointly paid their bills, Tom and Claire never had a real conversation about each other's finances. If they did, Claire would've known Tom had $55,000 in student loans at a 7% interest rate. The good news was that the loan had an income-based repayment plan, so the bill each month was affordable on Tom's salary. But what neither of them considered was if they got married, Claire's income would be counted towards his, and Tom's student loan bill would have *increased by $500 a month.*

- Claire didn't know Tom had no money in savings. After paying his car payment, the rent, and his student loan bill, Tom didn't have much left each pay period to save. And although he intended to spend $10,000 on her engagement ring, his only option was to use his credit card and slowly pay the balance off. Neither of them realized that adding $10,000 to Tom's already high credit card balance would have lowered his credit score. This could also have a negative effect on their mortgage application. But none of these things were on their radar.

- Claire had grown up differently than Tom. As a result of her parents' solid financial planning, Claire graduated from college with no debt. She also had a small investment account, which she inherited when her grandmother passed away. This was her emergency fund, which thankfully she had not yet needed to tap into.

When they sat down to talk about their goal of buying a house, they realized it wasn't the only goal they had for their future. They talked about their current jobs, their income expectations (career track, possible raises, and bonuses) and their plans to have children. This led to a longer conversation about how they planned to pay for college for their future kids and when they might like to retire eventually. Most of these topics were ones Tom and Claire had never talked about. In fact, they both thought they had plenty of time to figure it all out once they were married.

Thankfully, they were willing to have this life savings conversation. Together, they looked at income versus expenses. They finally shared how much debt each of them brought to the relationship. Tom had a lot. Thankfully, Claire had none. They discussed ideas for paying down Tom's debt while also trying to save for a house.

For the first time, they were totally transparent about their situations. Claire was surprised about Tom's student loans and had no idea Tom planned to charge her engagement ring on his credit card. Tom was unaware that Claire had an inheritance from her grandmother.

The good news was that Claire and Tom were reasonable people, which is often the case with young couples. They were also well-intentioned. They had goals, but they didn't have a strategy for accomplishing them.

After several candid conversations, Tom and Claire started to see how their short-term decisions would affect many important outcomes. For example:

1. Tom realized that putting the engagement ring on his credit card was a terrible idea.

2. Claire realized that the money her parents had planned to give them for a wedding fund might be better spent on a house down-payment.

3. They had no clue that getting married too soon would significantly increase Tom's student loan repayment.

4. They also learned from a meeting with the bank that improving Tom's credit score before buying a home would help them qualify for a much lower mortgage interest rate.

They decided to pump the brakes, build a budget and debt-paydown plan together, use some of the inherited money to pay down Tom's student loans, and postpone the engagement until they could better afford it. They found an online tool to help them track their income and expenses. For the first time in their relationship, they had financial clarity and transparency.

If you're thinking of getting married, then congratulations! This means you've found the person with whom you'd like to spend the rest of your life. Before you combine finances, buy a house, and have a baby, or adopt a dog from the local shelter, please take the time to talk about money. Agree to put it all on the table. Most importantly, do some math before you embark on this gigantic and legal undertaking called marriage.

Mistakes That Young Couples Make before Getting Married

1. Not having a transparent life savings conversation before marriage.

2. Not being clear about family expectations in the short and long term (i.e. having children).

3. Not understanding the impact that filing jointly once married might have on your money in the short and long term.

4. Not getting clear about debt and credit scores before legally tying the knot.

What You Need to Know before You Get Married

- Get a full inventory of each person's debt, student loans, income, bonus potential, expenses, employee benefits, and other obligations.
- Get an updated credit score for each of you from a credible source. Then, go through the report closely to be sure that it is accurate. If not, work to fix mistakes and clean up old data before you attempt to apply for a mortgage. This could really improve your outcome.
- Understand what happens to your tax bracket when you go from single to married filing jointly. (An accountant can be very helpful here.)
- Understand which of you has the better health insurance coverage at work and who should carry it. What are the out-of-pocket expenses or annual deductibles? How much

does it cost for a single versus a double versus a family plan?

- Speaking of benefits, do you have an HSA or FSA? Learn what these are and why they're so helpful. The sooner you understand your employee benefits, the sooner you'll take advantage of what your employer does or doesn't offer and begin to get yourselves on track for the future.

- Understand what you have for a retirement plan at work and when you are eligible for it. What if one of you has an employer match and the other doesn't? Should you add pre-tax or after-tax money? How might these choices affect your tax bracket? Will it be different now versus when you are married?

- Get clear about what you would want for the other person if one of you dies or becomes sick and cannot work. Proper insurance planning (life insurance, disability insurance, and liability insurance) are so important. Often, the younger and healthier you are, the less they cost.

- If you're married, does your new spouse become liable for your student loan debt if you pass away?
- Understand that if you have student loans repayable based on income, getting married could increase your monthly student loan bill significantly. Find this out in advance of marriage.
- Ask each other: What do you have for credit card debt? What are the interest rates? For how long? What's your current credit score? When was the last time you checked your credit report? How long before your credit card debt is paid off?
- Be sure to ask if there are any family members you plan to care for now or in the future. If your future husband intends to have his parents live with you in their later years, that might be good to know now.
- To the extent possible, and as early as you can, understand your parents' financial situation. Do they have a financial plan? Are they doing enough to save for retirement? Have they properly planned for potential long-term care costs? Do they have an up-

dated will? Who is their financial profession-al? If they don't have an advisor, it might make sense to find one. And if they *do* have a trusted advisor, should *you* be meeting with that advisor as well? When one finan-cial professional can coordinate a plan for multiple generations, this often makes a lot of sense and can provide continuity for ev-eryone.

Talking with Each Other about Money Can Be Difficult.

But remember, *not* talking about it (and then uncovering undisclosed financial secrets after the wedding) can be much, much worse.

A conversation with each other can be one of the most important early investments you make in your relationship. And the sooner you do it, the better off you (and your bank accounts) will be.

CHAPTER FIVE

TALKING WITH YOUR GROWN CHILDREN BEFORE THEY TIE THE KNOT

Jean and George were planning for their daughter Claire's wedding. Claire was in love with Tom and pretty determined to have the wedding of her dreams. She shared with her parents some of the lavish details she had in mind: renting a gigantic tent and having the wedding in her parents' backyard. This plan required caterers, a wedding planner, renting tables and chairs and dishes and glasses, and installing a temporary hardwood floor for the dancing.

Claire also had a Pinterest board with many ideas for floral arrangements and beach-themed tablescapes. She wanted an open bar with signature cocktails, and everything was going to match the theme of a Cape Cod lobster bake. This meant bringing in lobsters and oysters and clam chowder to their home in the Midwest (which was not exactly close to the ocean). Between the hired help and the prep and the rentals, the night was going to cost approximately $100,000.

To their credit, Jean and George had been planning for a wedding long before Claire had met Tom. With the guidance of their financial professional, the parents of the bride had set aside funds separate from their retirement. They knew they could afford a budget of $50,000 without jeopardizing their plan. But the thought of Claire spending $50,000 on one night for one lobster dinner seemed completely crazy to them.

It Was Time for a Candid Conversation

Jean and George set up a time to sit down and talk with Claire. George shared with Claire that he and Jean had saved $50,000, and this was what they intended to give her and Tom for their wedding gift. She could use it for the wedding and festivities if she chose to, but that was the extent of what they were willing to give.

This was news to Claire. She was their one-and-only daughter. Given the nice lifestyle her parents seemed to have, Claire never thought there'd be a limit on what she could spend for her big day.

Jean and George shared candidly they had planned for decades for many different financial goals: Claire's college tuition, family vacations over the years, and, most importantly, their upcoming retirement. They confidently explained the $50,000 for the wedding gift would come with no strings attached. If she chose to spend it all on her big day, that was completely up to her and Tom.

But then, Jean and George did something very wise. They took the moment as an opportunity to ask some good questions and discuss a few other ideas they guessed Claire might not have been considering.

George asked the first tough question. If the wedding budget was $50,000 and Claire was planning a $100,000 event, where was the other

$50,000 going to come from? Were Claire and Tom going to use their money for this?

Claire listened to her parents' questions and ideas. She knew from her recent financial conversations with Tom that he didn't have any savings. Claire herself had the small inheritance from her grandmother, but they were going to use that for Tom's student loans. Clearly, the young couple didn't have the resources to fund such a lavish wedding without going into debt. Claire knew this to be true. She kept listening. This time, her mom chimed in.

Jean gently suggested that she could help Claire rethink the wedding. With some creative planning, Claire might opt for a tasteful but less expensive event. Jean suggested ways to scale back on some of the pricey details. Maybe Claire could find a venue rather than having to rent everything for a backyard wedding? What if they stayed within their $50k budget, only used the parent's allotted money, and didn't jeopardize any of their financial goals by not pitching in for the wedding?

George took the conversation a step further. "Claire, I know you have big dreams for your wedding. But I also know you have other goals. You and

Tom have mentioned that you want to purchase a house. What if you spent half of the $50,000 on a wedding and used the other half for a house down-payment?"

Jean and George's ideas were practical and wise. Claire was intrigued. It really inspired her to think differently about a lavish wedding. It started to seem less important.

Claire went home to talk with Tom. He found the options to be freeing, practical, and smart. He and Claire talked about how much impact $25,000 could have on their plan. They reviewed his student loans and low credit score and how hard they were working to save money for a house down-payment anyway. They talked about the impact that her parent's gift could have on their future and how this influx of cash could accelerate their ability to buy a house much sooner.

Sometimes Parents Simply Need to Plant the Seed

Before your son or daughter moves forward with fancy wedding plans, it's important they know what the parameters are in terms of your financial support. If you're clear about your budget *and stick to it,* you're teaching your child an important lesson about planning, saving, and making good financial choices. *This matters.*

Paying for a wedding may seem like a big burden. What kind of expectations do your children already have about it? And consider for some parents, this might be the first of many challenging conversations they will need to have. What if I told you that Jean and George have a lake house, and they want to be sure

> **IF YOU'RE CLEAR ABOUT YOUR BUDGET *AND STICK TO IT*, YOU'RE TEACHING YOUR CHILD AN IMPORTANT LESSON ABOUT PLANNING, SAVING, AND MAKING GOOD FINANCIAL CHOICES.**

it remains in their family no matter what? This meant they need their future son-in-law, Tom, to sign a prenuptial agreement before he marries Claire. When is the right time to bring *this* up? Prenuptial agreement conversations can be extremely emotional and difficult to discuss. And the person bringing up the subject comes across as the pessimist.

There's also the difficult conversation to have about trusts, inheritance, and divorce. Jean and

George still need to talk with Claire and her sister about the fact they recently established a trust through their attorney. This trust was set up to name them as the beneficiaries of their estate when they die and to ensure that none of their family money ends up in Claire or her sister's ex-husband's hands if either of them gets divorced in the future. Awkward as it is, now is the time to have this life savings conversation as well.

Rarely do parents feel well-equipped to handle any of these discussions. Having clear and candid conversations take practice. When it comes time to have life savings conversations with your grown children but you aren't sure where to begin, you may want to set up a family meeting. Before the meeting, let the participants know your intention for the conversation and the subjects you would like to discuss. This way, no one is blind-sided by a prenuptial conversation or any other delicate topic. You may even consider gathering in a neutral place for the conversation.

As you've heard before, there's no right or wrong way to handle the pre-marriage life savings conversation. But *not* handling it can be problematic. Every family has different resources, issues, and dynamics. Your job is to find a happy medium between your feelings and your resources, then share these important thoughts and lessons with your children in a clear and honest way.

CHAPTER SIX

THE CONVERSATION TO HAVE BEFORE GETTING DIVORCED

I remember the morning I received a call from a long-time client. Mandy asked me to email her a list of all of her and her husband's investments, insurance policies, a detailed listing of who was the owner of each account, and to also include details of the kids' college accounts. And then she asked that we not copy her husband when we send her the email. Her voice was shaky. She didn't sound like her usual positive self, and I knew something was up.

This type of phone call in our business is often an indicator that divorce might be on the horizon. Everyone knows that marriages don't always last a lifetime. In fact, more than half will end in divorce. If this is your situation, please know that you don't have to figure out your finances alone. We often hear people describe their divorce experience as being lonely, devastating, broken, betrayed, and *feeling screwed.*

This does not have to be you.

In fact, having the right conversations with the right advisors will allow you to feel educated, calm, clear, strong, and empowered to take the next steps—even if it means ultimately divorcing your spouse.

I'm not saying it's going to be easy. Divorce is never easy for anyone, no matter how amicable. You're breaking apart a relationship with each other. You're ending relationships with your in-laws and each other's families. Your children's world will be turned upside down, at least for a period of time. The details can really be overwhelming—and this is before you figure out how you are going to divide all assets and tangible property.

Divorce is a gigantic undertaking. If you don't know a few important tips, it can also cost you financially *and* emotionally.

Money is powerful. You might not want to believe it, and you might not like it, but it's true—especially in divorce. When it comes to dividing the money, even the most even-keel people can go from zero to crazy. I've witnessed what happens to rational people when they become *completely irrational* during the divorce process. I've seen mild-mannered people become vindictive and nasty when they had to give up half of their 401k plan or pension.

I've also seen the sweetest of people get completely manipulated and ultimately agree to settlements they should never have agreed to. "If only I had more information up front," they would say afterward, "then I would have approached this so differently." Or "Had I known he was so attached to his pension I would have gone after the home equity and the investment account instead." Money is powerful, but knowledge can be an even stronger weapon in the divorce battle.

It is possible to get divorced and feel financially secure and confident when it's over. You'll increase the chances of this happening if you're willing to have three important conversations: The first is a conversation with yourself. The second is one with a financial professional. And the third is the conversation with your divorce attorney. This order might surprise you, but here is why:

First: Have a Conversation with Yourself

Yes, your first conversation should be a candid one with yourself. During it, ask:

- Do I have a sense of where our money is (bank, investments, cash in the safe)? Take inventory of everything.
- Regarding the house—Do I want to live here still if we get divorced? How important is it for me to fight for this place? Should I instead fight for the equity in the old house, and buy a new house so I can have a fresh start for me (and the kids)?
- How much money would it take every month for me to live? Consider the cost of housing, food, transportation, health care, tuition for the kids, saving for college, saving for your retirement, summer camp for kids, etc. Ask

this tough question: *What do I need every month to support my lifestyle now as well as for the future?* This is the one question that completely stumps people. Most happily married couples can't answer it, never mind trying to figure it out alone. And sometimes, you only have spotty information if you weren't the person in the marriage dealing with the money. The idea of starting over financially can be overwhelming. But getting clarity on your budget is imperative to ultimately negotiating your divorce. Trust me on this one.

- In the event of a divorce, if you and your spouse have been working together with the same financial professional, it's unlikely the advisor can continue to work with both of you due to conflict of interest. If you have a financial professional, you'll need to ask: Do I want to continue working with our current advisor? Is this the advisor *you* want to keep for *yourself,* or is it time to move on and build a relationship with someone new?

Once you can put pen to paper and start to find clarity around these questions, you'll be better prepared for Conversation #2.

Second: Have a Conversation with a Financial Professional

Often, I get referred to people only *after* they've already gotten divorced. At the end of the process, their attorney suggests they now need to look for a new financial professional. These clients come to me after the divorce has been settled and ask me for help in creating a financial plan for their future.

The good news is they've chosen to seek out the help of a professional with this very important financial project. This is often easier than trying to figure it out alone.

The bad news in my experience is that the client is doing it backwards. A settlement has already been agreed to. I know this might be a surprise, but in an ideal scenario you should meet with a financial professional *before* you meet with a divorce attorney.

The advisor can help you take inventory of your assets, help you understand what you have, work with you to figure out what you need to live on your own, and create a plan for you *in advance of any settlement*. Together, you can also quantify what you need to be setting aside for retirement, how much money the kids will likely need for college, and what your ideal housing situation would be.

A skilled financial professional can help you create a plan with your end results in mind. This is very impactful when the financial plan is goals-based. First, you'll have guidance in brainstorming what you want for your new future. Then, together you'll work backward

> **BEING EDUCATED ABOUT FINANCES CREATES CONFIDENCE. CONFIDENCE LEADS TO CLARITY. AND CLARITY LEADS TO BETTER DIVORCE NEGOTIATING.**

to figure out what you are willing and able to accept in the divorce. Then, and only then, do you reach a settlement.

This approach is powerful. Working with a financial professional helps you become more logical in advance of a court date or a mediation meeting. And remember, this all comes at a time when you're likely to otherwise be emotional. Being educated about finances creates confidence.

Confidence leads to clarity. And clarity leads to better divorce negotiating.

Here's why:

- Imagine you and your financial professional have already made the projections to know that if you receive 40% of your spouse's 401k in the divorce, your retirement will be sufficiently funded. When your attorney fights for 50% of the account, you'll go into negotiations already knowing you have 10% wiggle room if you need to compromise.

- What if you've already figured out that the new house you're going to purchase post-divorce will require a down-payment of $75k? When your soon-to-be ex-spouse offers you $50,000 equity from your current home, you know that number isn't enough. Now your attorney will know what you need to fight for.

- What if you go into court knowing that you're eligible to receive 50% of your ex's Social Security because you were married for more than ten years? That adds up to a lot of money and could positively impact your retirement picture. It's possible your ex might not be aware of this important detail. You can have confidence knowing this isn't something you need to fight for, and therefore, you can be freed up to focus on other important negotiations.

By creating a plan in advance, you'll know ahead of time what you're targeting. You've already developed your projections and plan with *your new future* in mind. You won't be the person who agrees to a settlement only to be surprised after signing documents that it was *not enough*. Instead, you'll go into the proceedings knowing where you stand, what you need, and what's worth fighting for. You also know what's *not* worth fighting for. And *that* is more powerful than just about *anything*.

Once you and your financial professional have confirmed what you need for your new future and you've worked backward to know what you need to negotiate, you're ready and empowered to meet with your divorce attorney for conversation number three.

Last: Have a Conversation with a Divorce Attorney

I recently received a referral to a new client from a local lawyer. He'd just settled the divorce for his client, Julie, from her physician ex-husband. Julie was going to be receiving several million dollars in settlement money. The attorney said to me, "I just hope it's enough for her."

I hope it's enough for her?

If her attorney is unclear that the settlement will be sufficient, Julie probably doesn't have that clarity either. To be fair, most divorce lawyers are not financial experts—nor should they be. They're there to help you negotiate the law and get your divorce settled in the best and most efficient way. It is the financial professional's job to help you have this life savings conversation.

Julie's lawyer's statement, "I hope it's enough" was genuine—in that moment, he really didn't know if it was going to be enough because Julie didn't have a financial plan worked out prior to her divorce.

It's not the lawyer's fault. In fact, no one is to blame. But it could've gone smoother. Julie simply didn't do her homework in the right order.

If you're going to get divorced, you're going to want three key people on your team: your divorce lawyer, your financial professional, and a great accountant.

The phrase, "I hope it's enough," is never a statement a recently divorced person should be left with, especially when it's too late to do anything about it.

Instead, get prepared. Get clear. Work with your financial professional on your budget. Have a professional help you with the math before it gets emotional and overwhelming. Build a financial plan with the end in mind. Understand what it's going to take for your new life to work. Ask questions. Get educated.

Each of these steps will build confidence. And then you can walk bravely into your attorney's office ready to fight for what you *are clear* you need.

CHAPTER SEVEN

THE CONVERSATION TO HAVE BEFORE GETTING REMARRIED

We all know that marriage is complicated. But second marriages can be *exponentially more complicated*. That's why it's so important that you understand the special considerations that people in second marriages face.

WHEN IT COMES TO FINANCIAL PLANNING, THERE ARE UNIQUE MONEY ISSUES THAT COUPLES ENTERING A SECOND MARRIAGE SHOULD CONSIDER.

Maybe it's your first marriage but not your fiancée's. Maybe you've both already been divorced, and you're bringing each of your kids into the new relationship. In every couple, the circumstances are different. When it comes to financial planning, there are unique money issues that couples entering a second marriage should consider.

Julienne is thinking of getting married. She is thirty-seven and has never been married before. She's been focused on her career as a cardiologist, and it's going well. Her finances are in the best shape they've ever been in. Her relationship with her boyfriend, James, is also solid. She gets along well with his two young children. She's ready to consider marriage. In their life savings conversation, they discuss the fact that James pays his ex-wife $900 a month for child support. This figure is calculated on James' modest income as a construction worker. Neither Julienne nor James realized that if James remarries, Julienne's high-income as a cardiologist might be included in the child support calculation, and James' child support payments could double.

Debbie and David are thinking of getting married. David's kids are done with college and both live independently. His alimony and child support obligations are complete. Debbie's daughter, Callie, is still a junior in high school and looking at colleges in another state. With Callie getting ready to leave for college, Debbie and David will soon be empty nesters. It seems to them that the time is right to tie the knot finally. But what they didn't consider was Debbie's status as a single mom and the fact that she's the sole custodian of Callie. Debbie is employed as a schoolteacher. Based on her income, Callie will qualify for substantial financial aid. But if Debbie marries David (a successful salesman), David's salary and bonuses might be considered part of the household income and could potentially disqualify Callie from financial aid. This was never something they considered.

Jenny and John are engaged. They first met at work where Jenny was a part-time receptionist, and John was an account manager. Jenny had been married to her first husband for fifteen years. He was a successful entrepreneur. In her divorce agreement, Jenny's ex-husband agreed to cover Jenny on his health insurance plan and to pay her a significant monthly alimony until his age sixty-five. What Jenny had completely forgotten is that both benefits would end if she ever decided to remarry. The health insurance and alimony together totalled thousands of dollars a month. Giving this up was something that would really hurt Jenny and John's finances.

Beverly and Bill were married for thirty-five years. Beverly was a stay-at-home spouse for her entire life. She and Bill made a lot of sacrifices over the years so that Bill could save up enough money in his 401k and retire early at age sixty-two. Shortly after his retirement, Bill tragically passed away. Beverly was devastated. She never thought she could love again. Then, she met Ted at a bereavement support group. They really understood each other. Their mutual companionship was exactly what they both needed. With their children's full support, they decided to get married. The family was so happy for them. In doing a little research, Beverly and Ted were both surprised to learn that the social security survivor benefits they'd each been receiving might terminate if either of them remarried. This represented a significant income. The thought of losing either check would create a huge void in their monthly cash flow. Certainly, they could collect their own social security, but this wasn't what they had planned for. Considering this factor, Beverly and Ted needed to create a new plan and decided to postpone the marriage until they had a better handle on their overall financial picture.

Carol and Craig were in their early 60s and approaching retirement. They'd each been divorced for more than twenty years, and their life together was terrific. They had no financial worries, lived in a beautiful home, and had accumulated significant retirement accounts. They were happy. But their marriages to their respective exes had really ruined their view of marriage as an institution—so much that they'd made the decision early in their relationship *never to marry again.* Fortunately, they'd scheduled a meeting with a financial professional to talk specifically about buying long-term care insurance. In that meeting, they were disappointed to learn that they wouldn't be eligible for the 20% spousal discount on long-term care insurance because they weren't married. That wasn't the only surprise. They also had assumed that if Craig predeceased Carol, Craig's pension would pay Carol a 50% survivor benefit. However, they were unaware that Craig's pension was only paid to a surviving *spouse,* not a long-term live-in partner. Without this, there'd be a big income gap for Carol. Lastly, they wanted to update their IRA's to name one another as primary beneficiary. They assumed that if one of them passed away, the other would be eligible for a non-taxable IRA rollover. What they didn't know is they were operating under the "spousal" rules, but they weren't married and therefore not eligible for those considerations. Although they'd gone into their meeting convinced that they'd never marry again, they soon realized that getting married made tremendous sense from a tax and benefits perspective. They decided to rethink their stance on marriage.

Before you *remarry*, consider these two important life savings conversations.

First: Have a Conversation Together to Ask These Questions

- When was the last time you reviewed all your retirement accounts? This is an opportunity to double-check your assumptions about your beneficiary designations. It's not unusual for someone to find out years after their divorce that their ex-husband is still named as the recipient if they pass away. Review these accounts in anticipation of your marriage.

- If you have children, what is your obligation to them financially? What about college costs?
- What are you paying (or receiving) for child support and alimony? For how long? Are there any stipulations or changes to that arrangement if you were to remarry?
- What do you have for health insurance coverage? How much is it? What are your out-of-pocket expenses or annual deductible? How much for a single versus a double or family plan?
- Are you still covered under your ex-spouse's health insurance plan? What happens if you remarry?
- What do you have for credit card debt? What are the interest rates? For how long?
- Do you have an HSA or FSA at work? Are you maximizing contributions to it? Should you?

- What does your employer offer for life insurance and long-term disability insurance? (Double check your beneficiary arrangements of all life insurance policies.)
- What is your current credit score?
- Is there anyone besides yourself that you might be financially responsible for in the future?
- What are your parents' financial situations? Do you know if they have enough money for retirement? Have they properly planned for long-term care costs? Do they have updated wills?
- If your parents could no longer care for themselves, would you plan to take them into your own home and care for them? This is a very important conversation to have sooner than later. Otherwise, it might come up unexpectedly after a health event when people are not as prepared to think logically.
- If you were to predecease your soon-to-be spouse, do you want your money going to him/her at your death, or directly to your children, or to both? Do your beneficiaries

on your investments or insurance policies or your will reflect these wishes?

This is a long list of questions, and initially, some of them might stump you. But the more you can address together, the better prepared you will be for your next conversation.

Second: Consider Meeting with a Financial Professional

Do you have a financial professional you both feel comfortable talking to? Do you still have separate advisors? Do you have separate accountants too? It may make sense to build your team together (accountant, attorney, and financial professional). They can work together to help you coordinate your plan and think about your future together instead of treating you as two separate people with separate situations. This will allow you to maximize all your options together.

I'm not saying you can't figure this out on your own. You certainly might be able to. Sometimes, however, it's helpful to have a third-party weigh in. An experienced financial professional can help pull complicated pieces together for you in a coordinated way without feeling like you're losing your independence. This is important for many people who've come out of bad first marriages or who've spent a long time rebuilding their lives after the death of a spouse. You can still maintain a feeling of control and autonomy while also creating a new coordinated strategy. If tackling this alone isn't getting you the results you're looking for, seeking out a financial professional might be a good option for you.

This Goes without Saying ...

But I'm going to say it anyway: This chapter is about a life savings conversation, not the *love talk* you should have before remarriage. I'm not suggesting that sorting out your finances is more important than romance, happiness, and your marital commitment to one another. However, taking on these complex issues prior to marriage can help build trust and clarity as you start your new life together.

CHAPTER EIGHT

THE CONVERSATION TO HELP DEFINE YOUR PHILANTHROPY

If someone asked you, "What's your philanthropic philosophy?" How would you answer? I pose this question to clients and friends all the time because I think it's a very important topic for us all to consider in our life savings conversations. Yet most don't know how or where to begin answering it.

I imagine you have organizations and causes you're passionate about, but most people cannot clearly articulate a vision for their philanthropy. In fact, most people's giving is not very well-planned at all despite how generous and well-intentioned they are.

Do Any of These Sentences Sound like You?

- I give to many organizations, but I don't really have a plan or a strategy.
- I give as I am asked, and then I'm always surprised at the end of the year at how much money I gave away. There are a lot of miscellaneous donations, but it's honestly not very well thought-out.
- I usually sponsor neighbors' walk-a-thons and local school fundraisers. I give to other organizations out of habit. I give $25 or $50 here and there, but I never believe that what I'm doing is going to make much of an impact. When I think about it, none of my giving feels very meaningful.
- I wish I could give away more, but I don't think I can afford it.
- I'm starting to feel like we give money away to too many different organizations. I wonder if we consolidated all that money and

picked one awesome organization who deserves it all, maybe we could make a bigger and more targeted difference.

- If I'm going to give money to anyone, it's going to my family first. Sure, there are lots of organizations who could use support but so could my kids and grandkids. I feel like I have to put family first.

Charitable giving is something many people wish they could do more of. It might surprise you, but there's a lot of generosity out there. People are often well-intentioned. They want to help organizations. They want to impact their communities. They want to make a difference. But they don't have a plan.

Does this sound like you?

What if you invested time to develop your own Philanthropic Philosophy? Doing so might help you feel more empowered, more inspired, and more ready than ever before to get into action with a *deliberate giving plan.*

WHAT IF YOU INVESTED TIME TO DEVELOP YOUR OWN PHILANTHROPIC PHILOSOPHY?

Here's a 10-Minute Exercise to Get You Started:

Step One: Divide a piece of paper into two columns. On one side, list all the organizations you've given to in the past twelve months. One the other side, list all the dollar amounts attributed to them. Can't remember all of them? Refer to your bank statements, your online spending app, or your checkbook register. Find every walk-a-thon and every Go Fund Me donation you've made in the past year. Write the organization and the donation amount on your paper.

Step Two: Add up the total number of organizations to whom you gave. Then, add up the total dollar amount of your giving at the bottom of each column.

Step Three: Look closely at all the organizations. Consider how each one makes you feel. Be honest. *Cross out the ones which don't inspire you.* Put a line through the organizations you give to out of obligation or habit. If they're uninspiring, then they probably aren't consistent with your passions.

Look at the list of remaining recipients. Circle the *one* or *two* organizations you care about *the most*.

Step Four: Think about the organization(s) you circled. What qualities do these organizations have that move you? Is it your local animal shelter, and you love supporting their work because it's the place you found your rescue dog or cat? Is it your alma mater, and you appreciate the education you received? Is it your church, and you were raised to give 10% of your earnings to support it? Maybe it's the Girl Scouts, and you're passionate about supporting organizations that teach girls how to be leaders? Define what it is about the one or two organizations you circled that matters most to you. Write it down concisely in one or two sentences.

Step Five: Look at the total dollar amount you gave away last year. Imagine if you gave all that money to the one or two organizations you circled. What kind of impact could that have had on the non-profit? What kind of impact could that have had on you? What if this is how you approach your giving in the upcoming calendar year? *More dollars to fewer organizations equals greater and deeper impact.*

Step Six: Take the total dollar amount you gave away last year and divide it by your annual income—not your net income, but your total income before you paid taxes. This will show you the percent of your income you gave away. For example, if you donated a total of $2,000 last year and your income was $100,000, then you gave away 2% of your income to charity. What percent did *you* give away? Does that percentage feel inspiring to you? Would you like it to be more? How much would really make you feel great? Write that down as well.

Step Seven: In one clear sentence, write down your Philanthropic Philosophy. Some examples might include:

- I give to organizations that support, grow, and develop women and children as leaders.
- I give locally to organizations that support the arts.
- I have chosen to give all charitable dollars to rebuilding communities in Puerto Rico.
- All my family's charitable dollars are given to support the missions of our church.

- My family has chosen to concentrate our charitable dollars to helping with food scarcity.

Once you have clearly written your Philanthropic Philosophy, what if you then decided to powerfully give only to those organizations that are a fit? More importantly, when you're solicited by non-profits which don't match your area of focus, what if you could politely and powerfully *decline* and instead you were able to explain your choice to consolidate your efforts into one or two specific areas? Your clarity and vision will inspire people.

If you work with a financial professional, be sure you let him or her know that you want charitable giving to become a more meaningful piece of your plan. Share this priority and ask for help building it into your strategy. Your advisor can give you current information about donor advised funds, gifting of your appreciated investments, and other strategies in which they are skilled. Once you have a clear plan, share it with your accountant and estate-planning attorney as well. Get your team coordinated and rallied around your generosity.

CHAPTER NINE

THE CONVERSATION BETWEEN YOU AND YOUR ELDERLY PARENTS

Penelope was concerned about her parents, Harold and June. While they seemed to be in good shape both physically and financially, she wasn't certain what their plan was. As they approached their 80th birthdays, Penelope wondered if they had enough money to last the rest of their lifetime. What about long-term care? If one of them got sick, did they have the right insurance in place? What about their funerals? Did they have those details all worked out? If not, should she do something about it? But she did nothing.

As the years went on, Penelope became more and more consumed with worry about her parents. Not to mention she was the oldest child and the one who'd ultimately be responsible for them.

But she didn't know how to bring any of these subjects up with them. In fact, it seemed disrespectful to mention death, dying, sickness, and money to her elderly parents. What if they thought she was digging around to find out about her future inheritance? Worse, what if her parents were struggling financially and didn't want her to know? Or what if something were terribly wrong with their health. Would she really want to know this? And would they even feel comfortable telling her?

The psychology here is fascinating and so common...

It might be surprising for Penelope to learn that Harold and June are currently working with their attorney on their estate plan. They're trying to figure out who'll be the trustee of their trust and who'll help make health care decisions if either of them became incapacitated. But they don't want to worry Penelope, their oldest daughter, with these things. They don't want to upset her. After all, what child wants to have a conversation with their elderly parents about death and dying? So, instead of upsetting Penelope and her brothers, Harold and June leave instruction with their attorney and their financial professional about their wishes.

Isn't this ironic? Penelope is worried about being impolite in asking these questions of her parents. At the same time, her parents want to engage in this conversation but choose not to talk about death, sickness, money, or post-mortem intentions because they don't want to upset their daughter. Neither party talks, but both continue to worry and wonder about each other.

There are many reasons why having an honest and direct conversation with your elderly parents is important. Without this life savings conversation, you miss so many opportunities to fix, change, or improve your family's financial future and overall sense of well-being.

Take Mary and Peter, for example. They're in their late 70s and in great financial shape. They have a son, Pete Jr., who's married with five-year-old twins. Pete and his wife are finding it challenging to save for their retirement while also trying to put money in college accounts for the twins. If you ask Pete, his #1 priority is paying for college. Pete's parents know this because he's mentioned it before. That's why they set up two college funds and gifted the maximum amount allowable into each of them. It's their plan to surprise the kids when they are in high school and let them know that their college tuition is fully covered.

Seems incredibly thoughtful, doesn't it?

It would be if Pete Jr. knew about it. But since he is *unaware* of this surprise, he continues to stress about not being able to save enough for college. He's even thinking of taking on a part-time second job to make more money to fund this goal. If his parents would be open to having an honest conversation with their son, it might save some serious worry. And it could create a far more coordinated and meaningful strategy among the three generations.

Then there's the Rose family. The parents, Lucy and Fred, are of modest means. In the end, they'll leave behind a house worth $500,000 with no mortgage as well as an individual retirement account (IRA) worth $500,000. In their plan, their two children are 50/50 beneficiaries of the home and the IRA.

But Lucy and Fred don't talk about money with their kids. They don't have a financial professional or an estate-planning attorney because they're so close-to-the-vest about their money. They assume everything will be split down the middle, fair and equal between their daughters. Marie is a school-teacher, and JoJo is a surgeon. The parents haven't considered the fact that their girls are in two very different tax brackets.

Most parents are totally unaware of this and do not consider how important their children's tax pictures are in their planning. Because of this, most don't designate beneficiaries based on their kids' individual financial situations. With a little bit of transparency, families like yours could save a lot in future taxes.

> WITH A LITTLE BIT OF TRANSPARENCY, FAMILIES LIKE YOURS COULD SAVE A LOT IN FUTURE TAXES.

Let's imagine instead that the Roses meet with a financial professional and an estate-planning attorney. The advisor might suggest that the Roses talk with Marie and JoJo candidly about their intentions for inheritance because the 50/50 division of assets might not be as fair and equal as they think. In fact, the advisor might also ask the Roses to find out what each daughter's specific tax bracket is. Lucy and Fred reluctantly email their daughters asking for this info. They are surprised that both daughters have no hesitation replying.

As the advisor suspected, JoJo is in the highest tax bracket, and Marie is in the lowest. The advisor explains that the Rose's house could be inherited with no tax, but that the IRA would be taxed as $500,000 of ordinary income to the beneficiary. With one daughter in the highest tax bracket and one in the lowest, the advisor recommends *not* splitting the house and the IRA 50/50. Instead, he helps them designate the right percent of each after taking into account each daughter's unique tax situation. This candid conversation could save the girls more than $100,000 in future taxes.

The advisor suggests they get an estate-planning attorney's perspective as well. The attorney recommends their house be owned by a trust and offers other excellent long-term planning ideas. Despite their initial hesitation to meet with professional advisors and share their personal information outside the family, Lucy and Fred leave these meetings feeling informed and more confident about their planning.

The Rose family's situation might sound like your parents' story.

So, too, might the Fortuna's story. Ruth and Richard are elderly, old-school, and do not ever talk about money with their children. In fact, their kids were raised to believe that life savings conversations were private, and such questions were impolite to ask.

As is often the case with elderly couples, there came a day when Richard needed nursing home care, and Ruth was no longer able to manage the household finances. That's when the kids learned the parents had done zero estate-planning. Their house was still titled in their own names. Richard and Ruth didn't have any long-term care insurance. The cost of care over their lifetime became so high, they not only spent down their money and their home equity, but the nursing home ultimately put a lien on the Florida condo. The kids never had these conversations with their parents, but they fully expected someday to inherit both homes and the remaining money. Instead, they ended up with virtually nothing.

With some trust planning and a proactive elder law attorney helping them, this situation might have been prevented—or at least improved. The Fortuna's situation is common when parents' pride gets in the way of a strategic family financial plan.

Sooner Than Later, Have a Family Meeting

In your meeting, share your thoughts and concerns with your parents. Politely and respectfully ask them questions. Find out who their trusted advisors are. Ask if you can meet those advisors now so you know who they are. Find out if your parents have powers of attorney, health care proxies, and any other medical directives in place. If not, encourage them to meet with their attorney (or your attorney) to get these important documents in place.

Help them to take inventory of all their accounts, CDs, investments, pensions, safe deposit boxes, insurance policies, and important other assets they may have. Get clarity about their intended beneficiaries. Make sure everything also names a *contingent* (secondary) beneficiary.

Take the time to understand their wishes and desires. Help them pre-plan funerals if they haven't already. Share with them the final chapter in this book. It may give them some ideas and prompt their thinking about how important all of this is for now and for their (and your) future.

Most importantly, let your elderly parents know you're there to help. Getting older comes with increased worry, anxiety, and fear. Be brave, and reach out to them, but be resourceful and not bossy. You can be

> **MOST IMPORTANTLY, LET YOUR ELDERLY PARENTS KNOW YOU'RE THERE TO HELP.**

helpful but don't take over unless they ask you to. And then be ready if that is asked of you.

Coordinate a Meeting with You, Your Parents, and Their Professional Advisors

If your parents are willing, you may all be able to gain clarity on what's been done and what's still on their estate and financial planning to-do list if you organize a Team Meeting. You'll learn if your folks need assistance or if they're in fine shape. You'll have an opportunity to build a relationship with their advisors during your parents' lifetime—which can be much more meaningful than waiting until they're no longer alive.

If your parents don't have an advisor (or if their elderly advisor has retired or predeceased them) gently offer to help them find a new one. They may be open to this. And know they may be more open to an initial conversation if you're not present in that initial meeting. Privacy and dignity are so important to preserve, especially the older your parents get. Be sensitive to this.

Proceed with caution.

But most importantly, *proceed*. Waiting until it's too late is never good, yet it's what so many people do who are unprepared, unwilling, or unsure how to approach parents about these important conversations.

Here Are Some Ways to Open up These Subjects with Your Parents:

1. Write them a letter or email expressing your love for them, your concerns about their future, and the questions you would like to ask them.

2. Give them some options for how to respond. Maybe they'd like to choose a day and time to meet in person to talk. Perhaps they'd feel more comfortable writing a letter or sending an email back to you. And then, patiently await their response.

3. You know your parents. Maybe they treat all their children equally, and if there's going to be a conversation about their plan, they want everyone present for it. Regardless of how you feel about certain siblings, be willing to arrange that family meeting for *everyone*.

4. You know your parents. You also know there's one child they feel most comfortable talking to about their affairs. If that child is you, rise to the occasion and offer to sit with them for the discussion. As the family's representative, be willing to hear whatever they have to say, and help them tie up any loose ends in their plan.

5. You know your parents. If there's one child your parents feel most comfortable talking to and that child is *not* you, be humble. Accept the fact that your parents feel more

comfortable sharing the details of their plan with your brother, for example, because he's the oldest. As long as they have someone to talk with, the siblings should rally around that spokesperson and encourage the conversation to happen.

After Going through This Process with Your Parents, You May Have New Questions about Your Own Plan.

Follow through on these important conversations but also keep in mind that you don't have to handle everything alone. Maybe it's time for you and your spouse to revisit your plan, goals, and future. Maybe you've successfully done your planning yourself up to this point but would like a second opinion from an attorney, an insurance advisor, or a money manager to confirm that what you have still makes sense and meets your goals. Sometimes, it's helpful to seek professional advice to confirm you and your family are on the right track.

CHAPTER TEN

THE CONVERSATION TO HAVE BEFORE YOU DIE

Harold and June have been married for fifty years. They are retired and in excellent financial shape. Their three children (Penelope, Steven, and Luke) are grown and independent, and they are proud grandparents to seven grandkids. June is a very involved member of the senior center, and Harold golfs at the country club as often as his knee allows. They have minor medical issues, but nothing too concerning. They consider themselves fortunate.

Some of their dearest friends, however, are really struggling. Ted and Cathy had to leave South Carolina and move back to Massachusetts. Cathy's dementia is progressing, and Ted knows she won't be able to stay home safely for much longer. Their daughter is helping to look for an Alzheimer's facility closer to her house in Massachusetts where she can keep an eye on both of them. Then there's Margaret, whose husband Mel had a stroke last summer, and she is now his full-time caretaker. Alice needs a hip replacement. And Wanda's cancer is back.

These events and circumstances have prompted new conversations for Harold and June. One morning over coffee, June mentioned they should get their affairs in order. Harold agreed. Aside from some estate planning they'd done ten years ago, they hadn't really tackled anything else. Frankly, they didn't even know where to begin.

AT A CERTAIN AGE LATER IN LIFE, PEOPLE START TO WONDER ABOUT THEIR LEGACY, THEIR FATE, AND THE IMPACT THEIR LIFE HAS (OR HASN'T) HAD ON THE PEOPLE THEY LOVE.

Maybe this sounds like you? Or maybe Harold and June sound like your parents?

At a certain age later in life, people start to wonder about their legacy, their fate, and the impact their life has (or hasn't) had on the people they love. They begin to ponder things like:

- In the end, what will people remember about me?
- *Will* they remember me?
- Did I do enough for my kids and my grandkids?
- I don't want to die in a nursing home.
- I don't want to die alone.
- I don't want to be a burden on anyone.
- I want to stay in my house as long as possible.
- Why am I staying in this house when there is so much to worry about here?
- I should downsize, but how do I deal with all of these things I have accumulated? I don't know where to even begin sorting through them.

- I wish I could talk to the kids about this, but I don't want to upset them talking about "the end."

This can feel like an overwhelming list. Now, imagine there are also worries about health: becoming hard of hearing, becoming forgetful, the inability to see very well while driving at night, fear of falling, etc. Getting older brings feelings of isolation, lack of relevance, and loss of meaning or purpose. Have you ever thought, *What's the point at this stage in life? Does it really matter if I live or die? I don't want to burden anyone.* You are not alone. All of these thoughts are common, and they each create plenty of reason for reflection.

It's Time to Sit and Talk about Your Legacy

Below are some ideas to help you get started and prompt your thinking. You might want to take notes, jot important thoughts and feelings down, and even share some of these insights with your children.

Intentions for Each Other: If you still have your significant other, you'll want to have the conversation about the intentions you have for each other if one of you passes away.

- Will you stay living in the same place?
- Do you want your spouse to be the beneficiary of everything?
- Or would you like your children or grandchildren to inherit from you at your death instead of waiting until both of you are gone?

For Harold, he wants to stay in their home where all the memories still are. For June, she thinks it'd be too painful and would rather live in a retirement community where there are other people around to socialize with. This was new information when they shared it with one another! And they realized either scenario was going to require some planning as well as a life savings conversation with their kids.

If you are widowed or single, these are still good questions to ask yourself. Even more important is sharing your responses, your wishes and your intentions with someone you love: a sibling, your children, a trusted friend.

Beneficiary Updates: Someday, when you're both no longer here (or if you are single or widowed and planning for yourself), think about what you want for your loved ones after your death. Give some consideration to the beneficiaries you've named for your investments, retirement accounts, and real estate. Does your current plan still accurately reflect your wishes? If not, it's time to meet with your financial planner and attorney to update it.

Meaningful Collectibles: Have you given thought to your collectibles? Are there things you want specific people to have? Write those intentions down, and make sure your wishes are clear in your will. June had some rings and earrings and wanted each of her granddaughters to get something hand-picked by her. Harold had old Swiss Army knives and antique cufflinks he specifically wanted his grandsons to have.

Charitable Intentions: Have you given thought to your charitable giving? Maybe you have named your children as 100% beneficiary of your assets. What about the organizations or causes you love? If you knew your kids would be okay with it, would you prefer to see some of

> **IF YOU KNEW YOUR KIDS WOULD BE OKAY WITH IT, WOULD YOU PREFER TO SEE SOME OF YOUR ESTATE GO TO CHARITY?**

your estate go to charity? If so, then this needs to be clear in your plan. More importantly, you'll want to share this intention with your children. Let them know what you're passionate about in case they're unaware. This is also something you'll want to include in your obituary. It sure is more meaningful to have an obituary state, "In lieu of flowers, please consider a memorial contribution to the Westchester Senior Center, June's favorite home-away-from-home," rather than "a donation to a place of your choosing." This guidance can also be meaningful for those who are left behind after you've passed. They often want to give to something in your honor. Make sure someone knows what is meaningful for you.

Funeral Arrangements: Have you pre-planned your funeral? Do your children know your wishes? Harold and June purchased burial plots years ago but never went to the funeral home to work out the details. Both were clear they wanted to be cremated and buried side-by-side, but neither had shared that with their children. Penelope had no idea but was so relieved when she finally got clarity on her parents' wishes.

Obituaries: What about your obituary? Do your children or loved ones know about all the meaningful and important milestones in your life? Hard as it might be, consider drafting your own obituary as a gift to your spouse and children. At least list the important details that people might not be aware of. At this stage in your life, you might enjoy

> **HARD AS IT MIGHT BE, CONSIDER DRAFTING YOUR OWN OBITUARY AS A GIFT TO YOUR SPOUSE AND CHILDREN.**

going back and reminiscing about the highlights, dates, events, and people from the past. If you're married, the two of you could write your obituaries together. And if you're single, consider taking on this meaningful project with your children.

When Harold and June did this exercise together, it provided them with a beautiful trip down memory lane, not to mention they had details and recollections of things the kids never would have known. They tucked their obituaries, along with copies of their funeral arrangements and their letters of intent into a folder and left it on their desk where it'd be easy to find.

Carol, a widow, invited her oldest daughter Melanie over for dinner and asked her to help put an obituary together. Carol was eighty-four at the time, healthy, still driving, and living independently. She described herself as "far from death's door" but thought that writing her obituary would be something special to do with her daughter. She also knew that Melanie, as her executor, would be responsible for this down the road, and Carol wanted to save Melanie the future stress of taking this on alone. For Melanie, it was one of the most special conversations she ever shared with her mom.

Letter of Intent: This is something people don't often take the time to write but might if they knew how meaningful such a letter could be to a family. A Letter of Intent is written to your family, friends, and/or community and is shared with them after you've passed away. It can include everything from, "Please divide my Christmas village collection evenly among my children," to lessons and stories you want people to remember about you. Here are some examples to inspire you:

- *I've left behind a $60,000 life insurance policy for the four of you. While I can't control what each of you do with the money, it was my intention to give your families $15,000 each to finally take the trip to Disney together. I know we talked about it for years, but I never felt healthy enough to make the trek with you. Please use this money and enjoy an all-expense trip on me. I'll be with you in spirit! Love, Dad*

- *Dear Daughters, I'm leaving behind my IRA to you. You may not know it, but it's a very special account. Most of the balance that's left was from the money that Dad earned during his working years. This account provided us a very blessed life, and now I am leaving it to you girls. As my financial advisor will explain, you're required to take withdrawals from the account over a specified period of years. Promise me you'll use it and do something nice for yourselves! You're all such wonderful wives and mothers, and you're constantly doing generous things for others. It's important that you take care of yourselves too. Each year when you take your withdrawal from the account, remember how proud Dad and I are of you. Love, Mom*

- *Dear Hadley Day School, I want you to know that I've named you as a beneficiary in my estate. The education that I received at your school made me a more confident and caring person. I'm grateful that you also provided the same incredible education for my sons. Please accept this gift as a thank you from our family and use it to build the scholarship fund so that others can experience the high-quality education that we all had the fortune of receiving. Appreciatively, Gordon Smith*

What you ultimately leave as your legacy is important. It can make a lasting impact on people and organizations. Taking time now to have conversations about your intentions, your wishes, and your final thoughts is so important to those who'll ultimately be left behind. These aren't easy paragraphs to write, but they can be very special. They provide clarity. And they can provide tremendous peace of mind for you.

As you tackle some of these big subjects, lean on your professional advisors to help. Your financial professional typically handles beneficiary arrangements, charitable giving strategies, insurance, and investments. He or she can help you make sure your affairs are in order. Your estate-planning attorney and accountant can also help with details in your plan. You certainly don't have to handle all of this alone.

And lastly, it's never too late to review your bucket list. Your bucket list includes all those things you want to accomplish before you die. Are there still things you want to do in your lifetime? What would it take to *actually* do them? Share these thoughts

IT'S NEVER TOO LATE TO REVIEW YOUR BUCKET LIST

with your advisor, your spouse, and your children. Make the most of the time you have left. How cool that you could lead by example. Show your family what it means to set a goal and achieve it, no matter your age!

Doris always wanted to ride in a hot air balloon and did this in her 70s. Rosie had a dream of visiting the Vatican. When her kids found out about this, they helped make Rosie's dream come true by signing her up for a trip to Rome with her church for her 85th birthday. Robert wanted to memorialize his wife, Alice, with a bench in their local park. He was going to have his kids fulfill this wish after he died. But when his son Joseph found out about it, he had the bench installed as a surprise. Robert now takes his morning walk in the park and sits on the bench where he talks with his Alice each day.

What is on your bucket list? Does anyone else know?

While you're at it, give yourself the gift of reflection. Write down all those Bucket List items that you *have* accomplished. When you look back on your life, you might be shocked at the number of accomplishments you have had. Most people who go through this exercise and take the time to think back on decades and decades of experiences and events are left feeling satisfied and complete.

> MOST PEOPLE WHO GO THROUGH THIS EXERCISE AND TAKE THE TIME TO THINK BACK ON DECADES AND DECADES OF EXPERIENCES AND EVENTS ARE LEFT FEELING SATISFIED AND COMPLETE.

When you are done, leave the list for your children and grandchildren. Your "Bucket List in Review" signifies a life well-lived, and precious memories worth sharing. Do not underestimate this gift for yourself. And imagine the message this also sends to your family. Be the example of someone who lived life fully.

FINAL THOUGHTS

Like most people, you will spend a significant amount of time working hard throughout your career, making plans, setting goals, and growing your nest egg. Now that you have read this book, I trust that you have clarity and motivation to continue building your life savings, and also build *life savings conversations* into your plan.

Each of these important discussions—with your fiancée, spouse, young children, your elderly parents, and even yourself—will be an investment in your most important relationships. Trust that they will have a far-reaching impact on your family.

Someone just needs to get the conversation started.

Be brave and let it be you.

Made in the USA
Middletown, DE
20 October 2020

22455905R00075